JUST JOSE

GW00759853

The Funniest Jose Mourinho Quotes!

by Gordon Law

Printed in Europe and the USA
ISBN: 9781701644793
Imprint: Independently published

Photo courtesy of: Ramzi Musallam

Contents

Introduction

Jose Mourinho is one of the best and also most quotable managers of the Premier League era.

The Portuguese set the tone in a way only he can by anointing himself the "Special One" on his unveiling as Chelsea manager in 2004.

As Mourinho likes to remind anyone who will listen, he has gone on to lift the Premier League title three times and won numerous other domestic trophies.

On his way to glory, Mourinho has lashed out at players, pundits, referees and rival managers – and none more so than Arsene Wenger.

The two were locked in an entertaining war of words and mind games over many years as Chelsea and Arsenal battled it out at the top of the table.

One classic exchange had Wenger claiming his foe was "fearful of failure" and Mourinho responded by saying the Frenchman was a "specialist in failure".

The likes of Pep Guardiola, Roberto Martinez and Claudio Ranieri are among the other bosses to have felt Mourinho's sharp tongue.

But Mourinho has a humorous side too, coming out with bizarre analogies like comparing his squad to eggs and omelettes and famously coining the phrase "park the bus".

His honest observations, the ability to wind up opponents and all-round cockiness make Mourinho one of sport's most fascinating characters and I hope you enjoy this unique collection of his quotes.

Gordon Law

JUST JOSE

CAN YOU MANAGE?

"I have top players and, I'm sorry, we have a top manager. Please don't call me arrogant, but I'm European champion and I think I'm a Special One."
Jose Mourinho on joining Chelsea

"To those who say we don't deserve it: In my country we say, 'The dogs bark but the caravan goes by'."
On claims Chelsea were boring title winners

"I think I have a problem. Which is I'm getting better at everything related to my job since I started."
The Blues boss on his career progress

"I am the manager of one of the greatest clubs in the world but I am also one of the greatest managers in the world... Did you read any philosopher? You spent time reading Hegel? Just as an example Hegel says, 'The truth is in the whole', is always in the whole."

The Man United boss gets philosophical

"Nobody in this football world is perfect. I am nobody."

A typical statement from Mourinho

"It's difficult for me to live without titles. I need to feed myself with titles."

After winning the League Cup

"I am very happy at Inter. I am not happy in Italian football – because I don't like it and they don't like me. Simple."

Mourinho says it how it is

"If I want a quiet, easy job, I would stay with Porto. There is a beautiful blue chair, we were league champions, won the UEFA Cup and Champions League. There was God, and after God, me."

On arriving at Chelsea from Porto

"I would rather play with 10 men than wait for a player who is late for the bus."

On his managerial philosophy

"Training Inter, I feel like Robin Hood. Even Jesus Christ wasn't liked by everyone. What hope is there for me? It doesn't bother me if people hate me. The Interisti know the job I do for them."

Mourinho is confident in his ability

"What is that? Style and flair? The way people now analyse style and flair is to take the goals out of the pitch. It's the football they play on the moon and the surface is not good. Some holes. But no goals."

He values substance over style after his Chelsea team is labelled "boring"

"If Roman Abramovich helped me out in training, we would be bottom of the league and if I had to work in his world of big business, we would be bankrupt!"

Mourinho tells it straight

"I don't say we are a defensive team. I say we are a strong team in defensive terms, but at the same time lacking sufficient fluidity in attack because that will take time to come."

Shortly after his arrival at Chelsea

"I am Jose Mourinho and I don't change. I arrive with all my qualities and my defects."

On being unveiled as the Real Madrid boss

"What makes me feel special is that I am above all of this. You think I care about some bullsh*t I read? Do you think I care? I don't care. I don't care."

On suggestions he only cared about making Champions League history

"Chelsea have suffered in the last two years and it's no coincidence that this decline happened after I left."

The manager doesn't rate his successor

Q: "Why do you think Chelsea are the most abused Premier League side on social media?"

Mourinho: "I think because we are boring."

13

"The moral of the story is not to listen to those who tell you not to play the violin but stick to the tambourine."

On winning the title with the Blues

"I am more scared of bird flu than football. What is football compared with life? I have to buy some masks and stuff – maybe for my team as well."

After Chelsea's lead over United slipped to seven points

"Look, we're not entertaining? I don't care; we win."

On Chelsea's start to 2006/07

"My bad qualities are that I don't care about my image and because of that, I don't care about the consequences of what I say and the consequences of what I do."

The Chelsea manager doesn't give a hoot

"Like me or not, I am the only one who has won the world's three most important leagues. So, maybe instead of calling me The Special One, people should start calling me The Only One."

He wants respect at Real Madrid

"After 15 years, I'm an overnight success."

Mourinho at Chelsea

"I am prepared. The more pressure there is, the stronger I am. In Portugal, we say the bigger the ship, the stronger the storm. Fortunately for me, I have always been in big ships. FC Porto was a very big ship in Portugal, Chelsea was also a big ship in England and Inter was a great ship in Italy. Now I'm at Real Madrid, which is considered the biggest ship on the planet."

During his first transfer window at Real

"Pressure? Pressure what? Pressure is millions of parents around the world with no money to feed their children."

When asked about the pressure of winning a game after losing twice in a row

"He must really think I'm a great guy. He must think that because otherwise he would not have given me so much. I have a great family. I work in a place where I've always dreamt of working. He has helped me out so much that he must have a very high opinion of me."

When a journalist asked what he felt God thought about him

"It's not important how we play. If you have a Ferrari and I have a small car, to beat you in a race I have to break your wheel or put sugar in your tank."

The Inter boss reacts to criticism of his playing style

"It is my fault [that my record at Real Madrid appears modest]. I have won so, so, so much that it is hard to live up to those expectations. Eighteen coaches in 21 years reached five Champions League semi-finals. Meanwhile, the rubbish Mourinho got to three in three years."

Speaking towards the end of his tenure at Real Madrid that yielded a title and two Copa del Rey cups

"If the club decide to sack me because of bad results that's part of the game. If it happens, I will be a millionaire and get another club a couple of months later."

Mourinho looks on the bright side

"Any coach can come into my office, plug a memory stick into my computer and download my training schedules and ideas, but they can't download my DNA."

On being so unique

"Jealousy is the weapon of the incompetent and frustrated. It makes me rewind the cassette of my life and remind me who I was."

On dealing with rival bosses

"At the moment, football is full of philosophers, people who understand much more than me."

He swipes at critics of Chelsea's 'negative' tactics against Liverpool

JUST JOSE

OFF THE PITCH

"If they made a film of my life, I think they should get George Clooney to play me. He's a fantastic actor and my wife thinks he would be ideal."

Mourinho in typical form

"I advise players to surround themselves with people who don't idolise them. If we commit traffic offences we should pay the fines. And at the restaurant we should wait our turn like others."

He feels players should remain grounded

"I don't have a taste for having 10 cars."

The Blues boss isn't materialistic

"It all depends on my wife. If I am at home, yes, I will see it. But maybe my wife would like to go somewhere. I would like to see it – I like to see football and it is a big game. But maybe I will have no permission."

On watching Arsenal's clash with Man United

Q: "Do you believe in God?"

Mourinho: "I think more important is love. Love is what matters."

"If I go to a wedding, I don't go in jeans. If I leave my house for a walk in Hyde Park, I don't go in a smoking [jacket]."

Mourinho talks fashion

"What position is my wife in? Eighth, at least."
The Real Madrid boss after being named the ninth most influential man in the world

"The dog is fine in Portugal – that big threat is away – you don't have to worry about crime anymore."
After the police inquired whether he had proper health certification for his dog

"We want football players, not fashion models. Last year, Kevin-Prince Boateng had more hairstyles than goals."
He wants players to be more focused

"For me, [Ivan] Rakitic needs to improve his Instagram and his social media because in this moment this is very important and he is not very good on that, he is good on the pitch."

He jokes about Ivan Rakitic after he fell out with Paul Pogba over his Instagram activity

"I've only been to a pub once and that was to get cigarettes for my wife at 11.30 in the evening. I prefer bars to sit and drink tea or coffee."

Mourinho is not much of a boozer

"You look at my haircut – I am ready for the war."

The Chelsea boss after getting a short haircut

JUST JOSE

MOURINHO V WENGER

"Am I afraid of failure? He is a specialist in failure. I'm not. So if one supposes he's right and I'm afraid of failure, it's because I don't fail many times. So maybe he's right. I'm not used to failing. But the reality is he's a specialist because, eight years without a piece of silverware, that's failure. If I do that in Chelsea, eight years, I leave and don't come back."

The Chelsea manager hits back at Arsene Wenger who claimed he has a fear of failure

"He was coming to my technical area and he was not coming for the right reasons. He was not coming to give some tactical instructions."

After being pushed by Wenger during Chelsea's 2-0 win over the Gunners

"Wenger has a real problem with us and I think he is what you call in England a voyeur. He is someone who likes to watch other people. There are some guys who, when they are at home, have this big telescope to look into the homes of other people and see what is happening. Wenger must be one of them – it is a sickness. He speaks, speaks, speaks about Chelsea."

The Chelsea boss makes a big accusation

"Unlike Arsenal, we sought success and tried to build it through a concept of the game using English players."

The Blues manager attacks Wenger's recruitment policy

"[Arsene] Wenger complaining is normal because he always does. Normally he should be happy that Chelsea sold a player like Juan Mata, but this is a little bit his nature. I think what is not fair is that his team always has the best days to play."

Mourinho responds to suggestions from Wenger that Chelsea selling Mata to Man United was unfair

"Many great managers have never won the Champions League – a big example is not far from us."

The manager has yet another swipe at Wenger

"Can you imagine if I said to Roman Abramovich at Chelsea, 'Please give me five years and I will try to win you one trophy?'"

The Real boss barbs at Wenger from Spain

"It's not easy. If it was easy, you wouldn't lose 3-1 at home to Monaco [in Arsenal's Champions League last-16 tie]."

The Chelsea boss replies to Wenger's claim that "it is easy to defend" in Europe

"I could approach this job in a defensive point of view by saying, 'The last three years the best we did was fourth and an FA Cup'."

The United manager has a pop at Wenger

"I'm not surprised, I'm not surprised. Me charged? Charged? If it was me it would have been a stadium ban."

The Chelsea boss responds to reporters when it's suggested Wenger could be charged for shoving him

"There are some managers, the last time they won a title was 10 years ago, the last time I won was a year ago. I will never be able to work without success… to finish fourth is not the aim."

Mourinho trolls Wenger as United manager

"If you add up the amounts the clubs have spent in the last three or four years I think maybe you will find a surprise. Get a calculator. That is one of the easiest things to do. It leaves no space for speculation. If you want to be honest, objective and pragmatic, it is the easiest job for a manager or a journalist to do. They have bought a fantastic goalkeeper and that is a position which is very important in a team. If you put Ozil, plus Sanchez, plus Chambers, plus Debuchy you will maybe find a surprise."

The Chelsea manager jabs at Wenger for his levels of spending

"The English like statistics a lot. Do they know that Arsene Wenger has only 50 per cent of wins in the English league?"

Mourinho even uses stats to have a dig at the Frenchman

"You know, they like to cry. That's tradition. But I prefer to say, and I was telling it to the fourth official, that English people – Frank Lampard, for example – would never provoke a situation like that."

Chelsea's manager accuses Wenger's Arsenal of having a "tradition of crying"

"At Stamford Bridge, we have a file of quotes from Mr Wenger about Chelsea Football Club in the last 12 months – it is not a file of five pages. It is a file of 120 pages."

The Chelsea manager would be happy to see Arsene Wenger in court

"The last time I won a title was one year ago. It wasn't 10 years ago, 15 years ago. One year ago. So if I have a lot to prove, imagine the others."

Mourinho takes a swipe at Wenger in his first United press conference

JUST JOSE

PLAYER POWER

"[Iker] Casillas? I have no problem with him. I like Diego Lopez more. And I have that right. Just as if Iker likes Pellegrini more than me. While I'm Real Madrid coach, Diego Lopez will always play. Once and for all, let's see if you can understand. I am a football coach. I was hired to coach football and a football coach has the power, among other things, to choose who plays. For me, I like Diego Lopez as a goalkeeper more so than Iker Casillas. I am not harming anyone. I like him better."

Mourinho fell out with Real star Iker Casillas

"They have to enjoy playing for me and Chelsea, but they don't have to be in love with me."

Mourinho on working with players

"The problem with Chelsea is I lack a striker. I have [Samuel] Eto'o but he is 32 years old, maybe 35, who knows?"

Mourinho questions the striker's age

"Some newspapers do great with Photoshop. Now they don't need Photoshop. They have the real pic."

After Eto'o celebrated his goal against Spurs pretending to be an old man

"Who were Lampard, Terry and Drogba two years ago? They were certainly not world stars. And in this moment who are they?"

On developing his Chelsea stars

"I always think there's our age in ID terms but then there's our real age because for me the real age is not the age on your ID. That's just a date when you were born."

The United boss on Zlatan Ibrahimovic still performing in his twilight years

"What is burn out? Is that when you are exposed to the sun?"

After Liverpool's Raheem Sterling said he was too tired ahead of England's match against Estonia

"Goalscorer, winner and funny."

Describing Ibrahimovic in three words

"Makelele is not a football player – Makelele is a slave. He's played the biggest game you can, the World Cup Final, and now wants to retire. But the coach told us if he is not playing for France, he is not playing for Chelsea. We know the rules. You are a slave, you have no human rights."

Mourinho is angry at France boss Raymond Domenech for taking Chelsea's Claude Makelele out of retirement

"I am no longer Chelsea coach and I do not have to defend them anymore, so I think it is correct if I say Drogba is a diver."

During his spell as Inter Milan manager, Mourinho changes his view of Drogba

"It's not even a game between me and him. It's a game where a kid made some statements not showing maturity and respect. Maybe [it's his] education, difficult childhood, no education, maybe [it is] the consequence of that."

Mourinho on Cristiano Ronaldo – before they made up

"I think it is Gerrard's loss more than Chelsea's. He can say, 'I was European champion at Liverpool' and I have to say that is correct. But I can say to him in the next 10 years we will compare trophies at Chelsea and trophies at Liverpool. And he will lose."

On Steven Gerrard's decision to turn down a move to Stamford Bridge

"Ricardo Carvalho seems to have problems understanding things, maybe he should have an IQ test, or go to a mental hospital or something."

After Ricardo Carvalho was upset Mourinho didn't start him

"I could write a book of 200 pages of my two years at Inter with Mario Balotelli at Inter. It wouldn't be a drama, but a comedy."

On his time managing the striker

"I wanted to kill the guy. He broke the rule."

After coach Silvino Louro celebrated the Manchester City result on the team bus despite being told to keep it quiet

JUST JOSE

MEDIA MATTERS

"I always wanted to coach a big club in Italy. The job at Inter is a big challenge for me. And I do believe it could be very entertaining for the journalists."

After being appointed Inter Milan manager

"The press don't go on the plane with the team? I'm sorry but I think that is correct. The press are not allowed in at training sessions? Correct. The press don't know the starting XI? Correct. I don't put your beloved children in the team? Correct."

Mourinho on dropping media favourite Iker Casillas from the Real side

"The English press, if you understand their philosophy, it was very funny to play their game. Salt and pepper every day."

Mourinho talks condiments

"Just to finish, do you know what was the result? This [holding three fingers up]. 3-0, 3-0. Do you know what this is? 3-0. But it also means three Premierships and I won more Premierships alone than the other 19 managers together. Three for me and two for them, two. So respect man, respect, respect, respect."

He demands "respect" before walking out of the press conference following United's 3-0 defeat to Tottenham

"Envy is the biggest tribute that the shadows do to the man."

He slams Jamie Carragher and Graeme Souness for criticising Chelsea's behaviour in the Champions League defeat to PSG

"I can tell you now, to stop you [journalists] from asking, that as long as he is not scoring, Shevchenko will play."

On Andriy Shevchenko's lack of goals

"I always win awards and I know why: I always win football matches."

After winning the GQ Magazine Man of the Year award

"Pundits are paid to wear my suit, but I'm not paid to wear their suit."

He attacks the pundits after Chelsea's draw against Southampton

"There I can be happy rather than have to pretend that I am happy."

His message to reporters that he will be celebrating his 51st birthday with his family

"Speak to your colleague about it, the one who has written the story. Organise a meal with that person."

The Real boss responds to a journalist who quizzes him about a story in the paper

"I have nothing, nothing to say. Nothing, nothing to say. Nothing to say, I have nothing to say. Nothing to say, I am so sorry, I have nothing to say."

Responding to four separate questions from BT Sport's Des Kelly after a 3-1 defeat by Liverpool

"You speak with Jamie Redknapp and he tells you everything about it. It was about winning – you have your pundits and Jamie Redknapp, who is a brilliant football brain, they can explain to you everything."

When asked to explain his tactics after Chelsea beat Liverpool 2-0

"Lots of people on TV, but nobody a Chelsea man. Carragher, Liverpool. Thompson, Liverpool, Redknapp, Liverpool. We don't have one."

He believes there is a media bias

"The thing I don't enjoy [about English football] is the way the media talk about us. I feel as if the knives are being aimed in our direction, while the flowers are in another."

Mourinho doesn't trust journalists

"You are not my friend, you are a journalist. If you invited me to dinner then I would not attend."

The Inter boss to a Sky Italia reporter who was critical of him

"When I go to the press conference before the game, in my mind the game has already started... And when I go to the press conference after the game, the game has not finished yet."

Mourinho on locking horns with reporters

"I am in the news every day. I think they really like my overcoat, they really like my haircut, they really like my face, they really like my behaviour, they really like to talk about me."

On being in the newspapers

"Would you phone the president of Ghana?"

When asked by a Ghanaian journalist if he rang Roman Abramovich to see how he was

"I think you need me to say something that will stop these strange questions. You want me to say, 'We are going to be champions'? Well, we are going to be champions. You have something to write now. It doesn't matter about the result against Blackburn or Manchester United, we will be champions."

To the assembled press after Chelsea drew their previous two games

Mourinho: "Maybe you should pick the team."

Journalist: "If you gave me part of the €9million you earn, I would."

Mourinho: "It's not nine, it's 11. And with sponsors it comes to 14."

The Inter manager's sharp retort

"At the very least we should be given a bit of credit and a little bit of space, and maybe the media should think we could help them discover why English teams do not win European competitions."

He wants respect for his Chelsea side

"Facing the press is not easy, but because you have to go, you have to try to take a lot of positive things for yourself from these face-to-face meetings."

On his managerial duties

"When I read a few things, I smell a few coats."

Mourinho on the press. Coats?

"When a dog three months old is the front page of a newspaper in this country, you cannot believe the things you read."

After he was arrested by police over a quarantine issue with his dog

"You could make noise with my silence, because you know the reason for my silence."

He ends his media ban in protest at Diego Costa's retrospective suspension

"There are a lot of poets in football but they don't win titles."

Mourinho says he got his tactics spot on as United beat Ajax to win the Europa League

JUST JOSE

GAME CHANGER

"I may look stupid saying this, but I think we should be going home with three points because we scored two great goals and usually, when you score two and concede one, you win the game."

After Chelsea lost their 100 per cent league record at Everton, with Didier Drogba's 'goal' incorrectly ruled out for offside

"What I'm about to say is not a criticism, I'm just stating a fact: there were no ballboys in the second half, which is something typical of small teams in difficulty. We intended to play like men and not fall on the ground at the slightest touch."

He labels Barcelona a "small team" after defeat in the Supercopa final

"Goals for are vitamins, goals against are an overdose of fatigue."

After United's 3-0 home defeat by Spurs

"You may as well put a cow in the middle of the pitch, walking. And then stop the game because there was a cow."

On Newcastle's time-wasting tactics against Chelsea

"My confidence is 100 per cent in Frank Lampard, but I told him if the next penalty is at a key point, then it's better for another player to take the responsibility."

The manager makes his point clear

"I found it funny because the left-back was kicking people and ready to fight everybody. I told Steve Clarke, 'He will kill him' and before I'd finished he did. Yes, funny."

After Andriy Shevchenko got roughed up by Forest's Julian Bennett

"During the afternoon it rained only in this stadium – our kitman saw it. There must be a microclimate here. It was like a swimming pool."

Before Chelsea's game at Blackburn

"In the first half it was very bad. On a scale of 1 to 10, it was −1."

On Chelsea's poor result at Newcastle

"If I lose against Bradford I say it's a disgrace."

Mourinho ahead of Chelsea's FA Cup tie against League One Bradford

"I feel ashamed and I think the players should feel exactly the same as I feel. It's a disgrace. A sporting disgrace, but it's a disgrace."

After Chelsea throw away a two-goal lead to get knocked out by Bradford

"If I made a mistake then I apologise. I am happy that I'm not going to jail because of that."

Mourinho was sent from the touchline by a policeman during Chelsea's Carling Cup Final win over Liverpool

"This is football from the 19th century. The only thing I can bring more to win was a Black and Decker to destroy the wall."

He is unimpressed with Chelsea's 0-0 draw against West Ham

"I wish them luck for their qualification match in the Champions League."

After Liverpool dumped Chelsea out of the FA Cup

"I am more than unhappy. Unhappy is a nice word."

Mourinho contains his frustration after Thierry Henry scored a quick free-kick

"99.99 per cent of the Liverpool fans think they are in the final. They are not."

After Chelsea drew the first leg of the 2005 Champions League semi-final

"The best team lost. After they scored only, one team played, the other one just defended for the whole game."

On Chelsea losing to Liverpool in Europe

"Mr Bonucci and Mr Chiellini could go to Harvard University to give classes about how to be a central defender."

On why his United side could not beat Juventus in the Champions League

"As we say in Portugal, they brought the bus and they left the bus in front of the goal. I would have been frustrated if I had been a supporter who paid £50 to watch this game because Spurs came to defend. There was only one team looking to win, they only came not to concede – it's not fair for the football we played."

Mourinho coins his now famous 'park the bus' line after Chelsea's 0-0 draw with Spurs

"Maybe the guy drank red wine or beer with breakfast instead of milk."

After a Sheffield United fan threw a bottle at Frank Lampard

"I want to give my congratulations to them because they won. But we were the best team. We didn't lose the game. Ninety minutes was a draw and it was a draw after two hours. We lost on penalties."

Reacting to being beaten by Charlton in the Carling Cup

"I don't feel very comfortable to tell you exactly what I think about the game. I prefer to be simple and pragmatic and say that we scored one goal less than them and we lost. I can't analyse with you certain aspects of the game, or individual performances."

The manager gets a bit salty after Chelsea lose to Stoke

"[Luke Shaw] had a good performance but it was his body with my brain. He was in front of me and I was making every decision for him."

The United manager is taking all the credit

"Every time I play Pep [Guardiola] I end up with 10 men. It must be some sort of UEFA rule."

Mourinho has a theory after Bayern Munich defeat Chelsea on penalties in the UEFA Super Cup Final

"One day, I would like Josep Guardiola to win this competition properly."

The Real boss refers to Barca's controversial semi-final win over Chelsea in 2009

"Look at the blond boy in midfield, Robbie Savage, who commits 20 fouls during the game and never gets a booking. We came here to play football and it was not a football game, it was a fight and we fought and I think we fought fantastically."

The Chelsea manager on a physical Blackburn Rovers side

"The style of Inter is the blood style, not the skin style. When you leave the field you don't leave the skin, you leave the blood."

The Inter boss salutes his team after they knock holders Barcelona out of the Champions League

"It was good – the attitude, the desire. We don't have A, B, C, D, E, F and G – but we do have L, M, N, S, O, P."

He describes United's display against Middlesbrough with the alphabet

"We would have lost if there were six Inter players left on the pitch."

The Inter boss after beating rivals AC Milan 2-0 with just nine men

"It is clear that I will end my career without having coached Barca."

After Inter defeat Barcelona in the 2009/10 Champions League semi-final

"At the moment, we cannot walk from the bed to the toilet without breaking a leg."

On Eric Bailly and Luke Shaw's injuries against Swansea

"One day somebody will punch you."

Mourinho to a Crystal Palace ballboy who spent too long giving the ball back

"I am a coach, not Harry Potter. He is a magician. Magic is fiction and I live for football, which is real."

After the goalless draw against Real Mallorca on his Real Madrid debut

"I understand why he [Sir Alex Ferguson] was a bit emotional. You would be sad if your team got clearly dominated by one built on 10 per cent of your budget."

After Porto's win over Man United in the Champions League

"Maybe I'm not such a good manager. And maybe the players are not such good players."

Reacting to Chelsea's home draw with Fulham

"Liverpool fans can continue to chant, 'No history' at us, but we continue to make it."

Mourinho baits Reds supporters

"There was a lot of commitment in Celtic's game, commitment, toughness and aggression. I'm tempted to use another word – but I won't."
After Porto's 2003 UEFA Cup Final victory

"We're not the perfect team and I'm not saying we are the best team in the world, but I think we deserve a little bit more respect."
On Chelsea's 4-1 win at Liverpool, having been accused of "boring" football

"I think we won that game against Liverpool because we scored and they didn't."
The Blues boss states the obvious

JUST JOSE

MANAGING JUST FINE

"It is omelettes and eggs. No eggs – no omelettes! It depends on the quality of the eggs. In the supermarket you have class one, two or class three eggs and some are more expensive than others and some give you better omelettes. So when the class one eggs are in Waitrose and you cannot go there, you have a problem."

Referring to lack of transfer funds being available to him at Chelsea

"Sometimes you see beautiful people with no brains. Sometimes you have ugly people who are intelligent, like scientists."

On the poor standard of the Stamford Bridge pitch

"When you play another team with the same qualities as you, normally the best one wins."

Mourinho on winning matches

"We are very calm. This countdown clock you have on Sky all the time, for us, there is no tick-tock."

The manager is happy with his Chelsea transfer business

"A player from Man City showed half of his ass for two seconds and it was a big nightmare. But this is a real nightmare."

He compares Petr Cech's terrible injury with Joey Barton showing his bum

"You like the ones at the top. They are so nice and so orange and so round and so full of juice. When you see a tree with amazing oranges at the top of the tree and then you cannot get there and you say, 'I got the lower ones because I don't like the ones at the top'. But you can't get there, so you say 'I don't want to go there' or 'I prefer the other ones'. I think it reminds me a little bit of that story."

The United boss explains how rivals City missed out on Alexis Sanchez

"Let's see if the sharks let us, because there are a few sharks in the ocean."

Mourinho is wary of the draw for the last-16 of the Champions League

"I am very happy because the club is beating records with the sales of new shirts. I don't sell shirts but there is a relation between shirt sales and the performance of the team. If we perform well they sell more shirts."

The Blues manager talks merchandise

"I would love an Aston Martin, but if you ask me £1million for an Aston Martin, I tell you, you are crazy because they cost £250,000."

He won't over-pay for a defender

"I am absolutely sure that we will be champions next season."

Mourinho is confident after arriving at Porto

"I am not concerned about how Chelsea are viewed morally. What does concern me is that we are treated in a different way to other clubs. Some clubs are treated as devils, some are treated as angels. I don't think we are so ugly that we should be seen as the devil and I don't think Arsene Wenger and David Dein are so beautiful that they should be viewed as angels."

The Chelsea chief on Arsenal

"Why drive Aston Martin all the time, when I have Ferrari and Porsche as well? That would just be stupid."

On rotating Blues trio Damien Duff, Joe Cole and Arjen Robben

"Young players are a little bit like melons. Only when you open and taste the melon are you 100 per cent sure that the melon is good. Sometimes you have beautiful melons but they don't taste very good and some other melons are a bit ugly and when you open them, the taste is fantastic... One thing is youth football, one thing is professional football. The bridge is a difficult one to cross and they have to play with us and train with us for us to taste the melon."

One of Mourinho's strangest analogies

"I hate to work with a big squad. It's like a big box of oranges and one goes rotten. A month later, you have to throw the lot in the bin."

The future's orange for Mourinho

"Everybody is crying that Chelsea keep winning and winning and winning, so I think that draw at Goodison Park makes everyone more happy."

After Chelsea's 100 per cent league record went at Everton

"The only force stronger than steam, electricity or atomic energy is human will. This chap Albert was not stupid. With will you can do things."

The Real Madrid boss motivates his players

"Chelsea are also a shark, but a clever one that knows how and when to attack."

The Chelsea boss had described Man City as sharks for spending £100m over the summer

"They make fun of Ozil, saying, 'Look, your father's coming' or 'Mister, your son's here'. Others say things like, 'Your son's much more handsome than Ozil and you'd never have a son as ugly as Mesut'."

Real Madrid's Mesut Ozil had described Mourinho as a "father figure"

"It is like having a blanket that is too small for the bed. You pull the blanket up to keep your chest warm and your feet stick out. I cannot buy a bigger blanket because the supermarket is closed. But I am content because the blanket is cashmere. It is no ordinary blanket."

On Chelsea's injury troubles

"Everybody was waiting for Chelsea not to win every game and one day, when we lose, there will be a holiday in the country. But we are ready for that."

On Chelsea's fine start to 2005/06

"I would need bodyguards in Porto [in Portugal]. If you visit Palermo [in Sicily, Italy], you probably also need them."

Speaking ahead of the Porto-Chelsea clash

"I think I have a naive team. They are naive because they are pure and they are clean. We don't have divers, we don't have violent people."

Chelsea are a bunch of good boys

"Beautiful, young eggs. Eggs that need a mum, in this case... a dad... to take care of them, to keep them warm during the winter, to bring the blanket and work and improve them. One day the moment will arrive when the weather changes, the sun rises, you break the eggs and the eggs are ready to go for life at the top level."

The Chelsea boss references eggs again, this time regarding his young players

"Two horses and a little horse that still needs milk and to learn how to jump. A horse that next season can race."

He insists Chelsea are a little horse that needs milk in the title race

"If we win, we go to the semi-final. If we lose, I will go to Earls Court and watch the wrestling on the 24th with my children."

He is not too worried ahead of Chelsea's Champions League quarter-final

"Everyone in the club must feel we have a good relationship between us. If Mr Abramovich wants to be in on the training session that's fantastic. Or, if at the end of the match he wants to go to the dressing room, for me it's great. It's never a problem."

When Mourinho met Roman Abramovich for the first time

"I want to push the young players on my team to have a proper haircut, not the Rastafarian or the others they have."

The Chelsea manager on shaving his hair

"If I play them in the Champions League, I want to go there and kill them – that's my message."

Mourinho on Chelsea after quitting Stamford Bridge

"In normal conditions, Porto will be the champion, in abnormal conditions, Porto will also be the champion."

The Porto boss makes a confident prediction

"After all that has happened this season – and that is a lot – I've reached the conclusion that I am a good loser."

After Chelsea concede the title to United in the 2006/07 campaign

"We have eight matches and eight victories, with 16 goals, but people say we cannot play, that we are a group of clowns. This is not right."

On Chelsea's start to 2005/06

"Everybody knows that the next round one team will play, another team will watch on TV."

The Real boss understands the knock-out phase of the Champions League

"We all want to play great music all the time, but if that is not possible, you have to hit as many right notes as you can."

He admits Chelsea aren't playing in top form

"Today I call them boys and not men. Because I think that they are brats and that everything that surrounds them does not help them in their life nor in my work."

The United boss on highly-paid youngsters

"If at the end of the season I'm leaving the club, you have the right to come to me and say: 'Jose, you are a liar'."

He wants to remain at Chelsea

JUST JOSE

BEST OF
ENEMIES

"We were together in my office. He asked me, 'What did you say to the press, young man?' We laughed, we joked, we spoke, we drank and when we go to Old Trafford for the second leg on Jan 26, it is my birthday. I will bring a beautiful bottle of Portuguese wine for after the game. The wine we drank at Stamford Bridge was very bad. And he was complaining about it. He is a wonderful, great manager. I have a lot of respect for the big man. I call him 'boss' because he's our [the other managers'] boss. He's the top man, a really nice person and he deserves to be the boss. Maybe when I am 60 the kids will call me the same."

The Chelsea manager on Sir Alex Ferguson

"I could say, 'What has he ever won?' But I won't."

On replacing Claudio Ranieri at Chelsea

"When you enjoy what you do, you don't lose your hair, and [Pep] Guardiola is bald. He doesn't enjoy football."

The Chelsea manager is alleged to have said this of the Bayern Munich boss

"I don't want him to teach me how to lose 4-0 in a Champions League final because I don't want to learn that."

After Johan Cruyff knocked Chelsea's style of play, Mourinho recalls the Dutchman's defeat to Milan as Barca manager in the 1994 final

"If they don't touch me, I won't touch anyone. If they touch me, I'll be ready to hit back even harder."

On Sir Alex Ferguson and Arsene Wenger

"We don't spend holidays together nor do we invite each other to dinner. But I respect the person and the manager.

On City manager Manuel Pellegrini

"If before a match I made my team watch Gladiator, they'd start laughing or call the doctor asking if I was ill."

The Inter boss laughs at Claudio Ranieri's preparations for the Coppa Italia Final

"I won't have a meal with somebody who has the same job as I do. And the only thing we have in common is the fact we're both football managers."

Chelsea's manager isn't interested in Roberto Mancini's offer to have dinner

"The only club where her husband replaced me was at Inter Milan, where in six months he destroyed the best team in Europe at the time. And for her also to think about me and to speak about me, I think the lady needs to occupy her time, and if she takes care of her husband's diet she will have less time to speak about me."

He goes in hard on Rafa Benitez and his wife

"I studied Italian five hours a day for many months to ensure I could communicate with the players, media and fans. Ranieri had been in England for five years and still struggled to say 'good morning' and 'good afternoon'."

The Inter boss after Ranieri criticised his coaching methods

"Maybe in the future I have to be smarter and choose another club in another country where everybody is champion. Maybe I will go to a country where a kit-man can be coach and win the title."

He fires a shot at Bayern Munich's Pep Guardiola after Chelsea win the title

"Academically he is an engineer and he does not need a calculator to work it out. Mata was sold for £37million, De Bruyne £18m. That is £55m. We brought in Matic for £21m and Salah for £11m – that is £32m. So £55m minus £32m is £23m. So for Chelsea in this window it is £23m – he does not need a calculator for this."

After City boss Manuel Pellegrini intimated that Chelsea had spent the most money in the Premier League over the last 10 years

"Because I don't behave as a clown on the touchline it means I lost my passion? I prefer to do it the way I do it."

The United manager takes a swipe at Chelsea counterpart Antonio Conte

"Bring an umbrella! And yesterday I couldn't believe that it was raining in the training ground, so it was great advice. The second advice was to bring my typical bottle of wine because now we are going to have many occasions to be together."

Advice from Sir Alex Ferguson

"Many coaches have won [the Champions League] more than once but there's only one club that was leading 3-0 in the final that managed to lose."

Inter's Mourinho takes a swipe at Carlo Ancelotti who was formerly with AC Milan

"One is a coach with a 30-year career, the other with a three-year one. The one with 30 years has never won anything; the one with three years has won a lot. The one with a 30-year career will be forgotten when he ends it; the one with three could end it right now and he could never be erased from history. This could be the story of a donkey who worked for 30 years but never became a horse."

On his relationship with Sporting Lisbon coach Jesualdo Ferreira

"Three years without a Premiership title? I don't think I would still be in a job."

The Chelsea boss barbs at Rafa Benitez

JUST JOSE

MEN IN BLACK

"Mr Roth has two ways out, apologise or it goes to court."

After being called the "enemy of football" by UEFA referees' chief Volker Roth. The Chelsea manager had wrongly accused Barcelona coach Frank Rijkaard of visiting official Anders Frisk at half-time

"It was no coincidence that he showed the red card to Sneijder. I have realised that they are not going to allow us to wrap this title up. But we were perfect. We would have won this game even with seven men. Maybe with six we would have struggled, but we would have won with seven."

He mocks AC Milan by claiming Inter would still have beaten them with seven players

"The only thing I have to understand is I'm in England, so maybe even when I think I am not wrong, I have to adapt to your country and I have to respect that. I have a lot of respect for Liverpool fans and what I did, the sign of silence – 'shut your mouth' – was not for them, it was for the English press."

The Chelsea boss was sent to the stands for provocatively putting a finger to his lips

"I know the referee did not walk to the dressing rooms alone at half-time. He should only have had his two assistants and the fourth official with him but there was also someone else."

Mourinho was unhappy Sir Alex Ferguson had words with referee Neale Barry

"If you ask me if I jump with happiness when I know Mr Poll is our referee? No."

Mourinho doesn't rate Graham Poll highly

"Newcastle are a good team, like Everton. At Everton, there are 30,000 referees, in Newcastle there are 50,000."

On fans influencing referees

"[Graham Poll] is good for games like these because he makes so many mistakes that people get angry and it motivates them."

After a Chelsea fixture with Man United

"If I tell UEFA what I really think and feel, my career would end now. Instead I will just ask a question to which I hope one day to get a response: Why? Why? Why Ovrebo? Why Busacca? Why De Bleeckere? Why Stark? Why? Because every semi-final the same things happen. We are talking about an absolutely fantastic football team, so why do they need that? Why? Why does a team as good as they are need something [extra] that is so obvious that everyone sees it?"

The Real boss reels off a list of referees who he claims had "favoured" Barcelona

"You can say the linesman's scored. It was a goal coming from the moon or from the Anfield Road stands."

On Luis Garcia's 'ghost goal' for Liverpool

"Congratulations to Mike Dean because he made a fantastic performance."

A sarcastic Mourinho after Chelsea's unbeaten home league record ended

"[Marcus Merk] is always against us. He must have been let out of prison to referee this match."

After Porto's clash with Deportivo La Coruna

"In other countries where I worked before, tomorrow in the sports papers it would be a front-page scandal. That's a campaign, that's a clear campaign."

After Cesc Fabregas had a penalty denied and was booked for diving at Southampton

"I am afraid of commenting. If I comment in a positive way I can be punished. If I comment in a negative way I can be punished. I have to adapt to the situation and that is to come with a very English answer, which is 'no comment'."

After Mourinho was hit by a third fine by the FA for comments that "bring the game into disrepute"

"How do you say 'cheating' in Catalan? Can [Lionel] Messi be suspended for acting? Barcelona is a cultural city with many great theatres and this boy has learned playacting very well."

The Chelsea manager on Messi's antics after Asier Del Horno was sent off

"People want a storm but there isn't one. I respect Sir Alex a lot because he's a great manager, but he must follow the procedure. I don't speak with referees and I don't want other managers doing it, it's the rule. One thing is to speak, one thing is to shout."

Mourinho on Sir Alex Ferguson

"I have to train with 10 men. How to play with 10 men, because I go there with Chelsea, I finish with ten. I go there with Inter, I finish with 10 and I have to train to play with 10 men because it can happen again."

Ahead of Real's 2010/11 Champions League second leg at Barcelona

"The circumstances are difficult for us with the new football rules that we have to face. It is not possible to have a penalty against Manchester United and it is not possible to have penalties in favour of Chelsea. It is not a conspiracy, it is fact. I speak facts. If not, I need big glasses."

Chelsea's manager feels a referee bias

JUST JOSE

A FUNNY OLD GAME

"The way the matches are in this country is unbelievable. The players either die or get better."

Mourinho loves the Premier League

"We are in the second year of trying to rebuild a football team that is not one of the best teams in the world. Manchester City buy full-backs for the price of strikers."

The United manager on the task ahead

"I saw their players and manager go for a lap of honour after losing to us in their last home game. In Portugal if you do this, they throw bottles at you."

The Chelsea boss on Manchester United

"I think boring is 10 years without a title – that's boring. If you support a club and you wait, wait, wait for so many years without a Premier League title, then that's boring."

He reacts to "boring" jibes by slamming Arsenal

"You can have a fantastic movie while respecting others. You don't need to be disrespectful to have a fantastic movie. You can be a rich club and buy the best players in the world but you cannot buy class and they showed that clearly, that was really obvious."

The United boss on Manchester City's behind-the-scenes documentary 'All or Nothing'

"I say to the fans that the fans are the fans and have the right to their opinions and reactions but there is something that I used to call 'football heritage'. I don't know if, I try to translate from my Portuguese, which is almost perfect, to my English, which is far from perfect – 'football heritage', what a manager inherits. In the last seven years the worst position of Manchester City in the Premier League was fourth. In the last seven years Manchester City were champions twice and if you want to say three times, they were second twice. That's heritage."

An extract from Mourinho's 12-minute rant after United exited the Champions League to Sevilla

"When the French players were on holidays in Christmas, we were playing five matches in 10 days, so don't speak with us about accumulation of matches and fatigue."

The Chelsea manager is not feeling sorry for PSG after they were hit with injuries

"I am not anti-Barcelona. I am coach of Real but Barca doesn't worry me. My only concern is to grow Real. Barca are great rivals and we respect them. If I am hated at Barcelona, it is their problem but not mine. Fear is not a word in my football dictionary."

Mourinho in his first Real Madrid press conference

"If Chelsea fans at Norwich are singing, 'Jose Mourinho' and the other guys sing, 'F*ck off Mourinho', I don't think it's aggressive hostility. It's better than them ignoring me."

He enjoys banter with the fans

"Liverpool are favourites because in the year 2007, we've played 27 matches and Liverpool played three or four."

Ahead of Chelsea's Champions League semi-final second leg

"When I hear them say they can win the title, it makes me feel like laughing."

The Chelsea boss on Liverpool

"That was not a football score, it was a hockey score... In training I often play matches of three against three and when the score reaches 5-4, I send the players back to the dressing room, because they are not defending properly."

On Arsenal's 5-4 north London derby win over Tottenham

"Barcelona have a great club. But in 200 years of history they have won the European Cup only once. I have been managing for a few years and I have already won the same amount."

Mourinho – shortly before Barcelona went on to win the Champions League later that season

"As for [Pietro] Lo Monaco I do not know who he is. With the name Monaco I have heard of Bayern Monaco (Munich) and the Monaco GP, the Tibetan Monaco (Monk), and the Principality of Monaco. I have never heard of any others."

The Inter boss mocks the Catania president after he claimed he wanted to "smack Mourinho in the mouth" after their victory

"A great pianist doesn't run around the piano or do push-ups with his fingertips. To be great, he plays the piano."

He believes a great footballer shouldn't perform the physical duties

"When [Chelsea] have somebody who wins four Premier Leagues for them, I'll be number two. For this moment, 'Judas' is number one."

The United boss hits back at a section of Chelsea supporters who jeered him

"Boring? I'd agree. I played against them 10 times and never lost."

Mourinho responds to the Arsenal fans' flack at the Emirates

"Places like this [Bramall Lane] are the soul of English football. The crowd is magnificent, saying, 'F*ck off Mourinho' and so on."

The Chelsea chief on English supporters

Also available

Printed in Great Britain
by Amazon